ye! *H*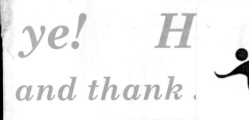
and thank ...

Our Generous Underwriters . . .

The Meadows Foundation
Wal-Mart Stores, Inc.
Bridgeway Charitable Foundation

Texas Bar Foundation
Donne Di Domani
The Luchsinger Family Foundation
Priest River, Ltd./LIT Group, Inc.
Good Earth Foundation
Moriah & Rod Crosby
Child Advocates, Inc.
In Honor of the Swalm Foundation
In Honor of All Advocates and Children
The Powell Foundation
Barbara & Ralph Zuckerberg
Charles & Sonja Novo
Houston Junior Woman's Club
Houston Young Lawyers Foundation
Winstead Sechrest & Minick, P.C.
St. Luke's United Methodist Church
The Trull Foundation
Congregation of the Incarnate Word
    and Blessed Sacrament
Judy & Henry Sauer
Kim & Scott David
Ed & Bernie Powell
Mindy & Blake Young
Kappa Delta Sorority
    Houston Day Alumnae Association
Mary Grace & Mike Landrum
Catholic Daughters of the Americas-
    Court Christ the King #1750
Peggy & Mark Heeg
Linda Murphy
Elizabeth A. Sauer

Ginya & Clayton Trier
Cheryl & Milton West
Marjo & Ralph Sauer
Alan C. Baum, MD
Kimberly Morris
Sherra Aguirre
JoAnn Droluk
Earthman Funeral Directors
Celia & Charles Holmsten
In Memory of Nicole Broussard
Gary & Elizabeth Ingersoll
Bobbie & Richard Kristinik
Ladies Auxiliary -
    Knights of Columbus Co. 2917
Ross LeFevre
Rosemary Listi
Cora Sue & Harry Mach
Nancy & Peter Thompson
DeLores & Fred Warner
Barbara Woolhandler
Dennis & Marnie Schaffer
Mary B. Dusing
Barrie & Larry Ewing
Kerry A. Sheppard
Roxanne Barton
Ana Eigler
Sandy & Bob Earthman
Lannie & Bill Bluethmann
Pat Glauser
Dr. Tom & Brigid Earthman

"My deepest appreciation goes out to each staff member, Court Appointed Special Advocate, Board member, Advisory Board member, volunteer, and financial contributor for your dedication and support of Child Advocates, Inc. and this project. Because of you, there are thousands of children who are given hope and a better chance to succeed in life. Your efforts, like this book, are our legacy for the future."

—Sonya Galvan
CEO, Child Advocates, Inc.
Houston, Texas

Just for Now:
kids and the people of the court

WRITTEN BY KIMBERLY MORRIS

WITH THE STAFF AND VOLUNTEERS OF CHILD ADVOCATES, INC.

ILLUSTRATED BY TONY SANSEVERO

Based on a Storyline by Kathleen Burke

child**advocates**®

Houston, Texas
2007

Child Advocates, Inc. mobilizes court appointed volunteers to break the vicious cycle of child abuse. We speak up for abused children who are lost in the system and guide them into safe environments where they can thrive.

Child Advocates, Inc.
2401 Portsmouth Street, Ste. 210
Houston, Texas 77098
www.childadvocates.org
713.529.1396

* * *

Creative Direction and Publishing Services by Publishing Matters

Digital Art, Art Editing, and Book Design by Ira S. Van Scoyoc, Emerald Phoenix Media
& Pam Van Scoyoc

Cover Design by Marty Ittner

* * *

Child Advocates, Inc. is the Court Appointed Special Advocate (CASA) Program
in Houston, Texas, and is a member of Texas CASA and National CASA

Project Coordination by Jackie Crowley and Barbara Abell

Publisher-suggested cataloging:

Morris, Kimberly
    Just for now : kids and the people of the court / written by Kimberly Morris with the staff and volunteers of Child
Advocates, Inc. ; illustrations by Tony Sansevero ; based on a storyline by Kathleen Burke.
    Houston, Tex. : Child Advocates, 2007.
    48 p. : ill. ; 29 cm.
    When Gilbert and his big sister Rachel go into foster care they meet a lot of adults who are there to help them – a
caseworker, foster parents, foster brothers and sisters, a lawyer, a therapist, a judge, their own court appointed
special advocate (CASA), and a dog named Spud!
    Explains the roles of various people in the court system; includes a glossary for such terms as caseworker, foster
home, attorney, court appointed special advocate (CASA), Child Protective Services (CPS), guardian ad litem (GAL),
therapist, etc.
    Spanish ed. published simultaneously.
    User's guide available from: www.childadvocates.org
    Intended audience: Ages 6-12.
    ISBN: 0-9754953-9-9 ; ISBN 13: 978-0-9754953-9-1

1. Domestic relations courts—United States—Juvenile literature. 2. Children—Legal status, laws, etc.—United States—
Juvenile literature. 3. Foster home care—United States—Juvenile literature. [1. Domestic relations courts. 2. Courts.
3. Abused children. 4. Children. 5. Foster home care.] I. Sansevero, Tony, ill. II. Burke, Kathleen. III. Child Advocates,
Inc. IV. Title. V. Title: Kids and the people of the court. VI. Title: People of the court.
[Fic] |22 *TxGeoBT*   LCCN: 2006930714

Printed by Grover Printing, a Consolidated Graphics Company
Houston, Texas, USA

Dedicated to abused and neglected children, Court Appointed Special Advocates, caseworkers, foster families, attorneys and guardians ad litem, family court judges, and parents who strive to make things right.

—Child Advocates, Inc.

This book was made possible by underwriting from The Meadows Foundation, Wal-Mart Stores, Inc., Bridgeway Charitable Foundation, and many other generous donors.

Mom had been gone for days. But Rachel wasn't worried until a strange lady and a **police officer** came to the door.

The lady smiled. "I'm Ms. Casey from **Child Protective Services**. This is Officer Garcia. Your school says you haven't been there in a week."

Rachel stared at them. "I'm not supposed to leave the house when Mom's not here. Besides, I don't need any protection. The doors and windows are locked real tight. And I haven't talked to any strangers at all . . . *except you.*"

Rachel wished Ms. Casey would take the hint and go away.

Instead, Ms. Casey walked in and kept on asking questions.

"What about your little brother? Who's taking care of him?"

"I am. I take care of Gilbert all the time."

Ms. Casey quickly packed a bag for each of them. "That's your mom's job. So until she comes back, we need to take you to a foster home. Don't worry. It's temporary."

Ms. Casey led them to her car. Gilbert climbed into the back. "What does temporary mean?" Gilbert asked Rachel.

"It means *just for now*."

Gilbert waved goodbye to Officer Garcia and turned around. "What's a foster home?"

Rachel helped him with his seatbelt. "Same thing I think. A home that's just for now."

"So are we foster kids?" he whispered.

"I guess," she whispered back. "At least, just for now."

The temporary-just-for-now **foster home** belonged to Mr. and Mrs. Lin. They were the foster parents. Rachel figured they must really like foster kids because they sure had a bunch of 'em.

Maria and Rosa were twins. They didn't know why they were in foster care. They didn't mind though—not as long as they had each other to play with.

Sarah was in foster care because her parents hit her. Ms. Casey was supposed to be finding her some new parents. Nice ones. But Sarah said Ms. Casey had been looking for a long time and wasn't having a bit of luck.

Vernon was in foster care because his mom and dad were in jail. Vernon liked to pretend he was SuperVernon. He said if he were really SuperVernon, he would bust his parents out of jail and fly them to Disney World.

A few days later, Ms. Casey came to visit and told them Mom was sick. Ms. Casey didn't say so, but Rachel knew Mom was sick from drugs and alcohol. This wasn't the first time.

Gilbert pulled at Ms. Casey's sleeve. "When can we see Mom? When can we go home?"

Ms. Casey replied. "That's up to the **judge**."

That sounded scary to Rachel. On TV, judges sent people to jail. "A judge? Is Mom in trouble?"

Ms. Casey shook her head. "No, no, no. In **family court**, a judge is the person who decides what's best for everyone—you *and* your mom. The judge will make those decisions at the **hearing**."

JUDGE - The person in the courtroom who makes the final decisions.

JUDGE / COURT - Sometimes when people say the court, they mean the judge.

FAMILY COURT - The official meeting place where grownups, and sometimes kids, gather to talk to the judge and make their families work better.

"When can we talk to this judge?"

"You can't. You'll be in school, a new school a few blocks away."

Now Rachel was really confused. "But how can the judge hear us if we're not there?"

Ms. Casey stood. "I wish I had time to explain. But I have some other kids to check on now. Don't worry. I have an idea. I'll ask Mr. Zapato to visit you."

"Who is Mr. Zapato?" Gilbert asked.

Ms. Casey hurried toward the door. "Mr. Zapato is your **attorney**."

Rachel and Gilbert looked at each other with big eyes.

Attorney?

What attorney?

HEARINGS - *Every few months, lots of grownups who care about you get together and talk to the judge about how you and your parents are doing. Those meetings are called hearings.*

ATTORNEY - *Someone who talks to the judge for you. An attorney is the same thing as a lawyer.*

Rachel and Gilbert waited to hear from Mr. Zapato. While they waited, they went to the new school. The teachers there didn't know anything at all about Rachel and Gilbert. They didn't know that Gilbert was an artist and that Rachel loved to play soccer.

They gave Gilbert work that was too hard, and they gave Rachel work that was too easy. The days went by, and just-for-now seemed to be turning into forever.

When the weather turned nice, they explored the neighborhood.

Gilbert found a lizard and a turtle. When he brought them home, Mrs. Lin said the best place for lizards and turtles was outside. So Gilbert had to let them go.

Finally, Mr. Zapato came to see them. He said he was their **attorney ad litem** and his job was to protect their interests.

Rachel spoke right up. "Then I'm not talkin'. The last time I talked to somebody who wanted to protect us, we wound up in a temporary-just-for-now foster home."

"But Rachel, I need you to talk to me. My job is to listen to what you have to say and tell the judge what you want. When I go to court, I'll be standing in your shoes." Mr. Zapato pretended to hobble around the room in Gilbert's shoes. "Ouch! Ouch! Ouch! Boy, these shoes are tight!"

Rachel laughed. "Then tell the judge we want to go home. Tell the judge we want to see our mom."

Mr. Zapato said that he would.

One day, Gilbert found
a dirty and hungry stray dog.
Gilbert named him Spud and
fed him two ham sandwiches
with cheese. He decided to
give him a bath and hide him
in the closet. So far, he'd lost
a lizard, a turtle,
and a mom.
That was
enough.

The other kids liked sharing the secret. It made them feel like real brothers and sisters. They used up all of Rosa's shampoo. Pretty soon there were so many bubbles they could hardly find Spud.

Rachel mopped up suds with a towel. "How are we going to sneak him out of here and into Gilbert's closet?"

Maria grinned. "That sounds like a job for *SuperVernon!*"

15

Vernon wrapped Spud in his cape and tiptoed across the landing.

Downstairs, Mrs. Lin sneezed so loud the whole house shook. "AHHH CHOOO! AHHH CHOOO! AHHHHHH CHOOOOOO!"

She wiped her nose. "That's odd. The only thing that makes me sneeze like that is a dog. But there's no dog in this house. AHHHHHH CHOOOOOO!"

Mrs. Lin sneezed through lunch. She sneezed through dinner. She even sneezed through homework.

That night Rachel gathered everybody together. "We've got to move Spud before poor Mrs. Lin blows the roof off. The shed in the vacant lot next door is a perfect hiding place. Nobody will ever know he's in there. Come on."

They made a leash out of Sarah's belt – and off they went.

Every day, before school and after, the kids took turns feeding Spud. They all saved a bit of each meal for him so that he would have enough.

After they fed Spud, they let him out for a few minutes to play. When they left, they slid a board across the hole in the wall so he would be locked in safe and sound.

The next time Ms. Casey came to visit, Rachel ran to greet her. "Well? Did Mr. Zapato talk to the judge? Can we go home now?"

Ms. Casey told Rachel that yes, Mr. Zapato talked to the judge. But no, they couldn't go home yet. She used a lot of big words like a **family plan of service** and **permanency placement team**.

It just sounded like a lot of blah, blah, blah.

Rachel stamped her foot. "You tricked us. You said this was just-for-now, but we've been here for WEEKS! Sarah has been here for MONTHS! I don't think you know what you're doing at all."

Ms. Casey sighed. "I know it's hard to understand. But give me a few days. I have an idea."

> *A FAMILY PLAN OF SERVICE* is a list of things your parents are supposed to do to show the judge they are serious about wanting to take good care of you.

> The grownups who work together to figure out where you will be safe and well taken care of are your *PERMANENCY PLACEMENT TEAM.* Your team might include your Court Appointed Special Advocate, or CASA. What's a Court Appointed Special Advocate, or CASA? Turn the page and find out.

Rachel didn't believe Ms. Casey had an idea. She didn't believe anybody anymore. So she was very surprised when Ms. Casey invited them to her office at Child Protective Services. She introduced them to a lady named Mrs. Hart.

Mrs. Hart gave them heart-shaped candy to help them remember her name.

Rachel put the candy in her pocket. "Do you work here?"

Mrs. Hart smiled. "No, I don't work here. I came here today especially to meet you. I'm your **Court Appointed Special Advocate**. Some people call me a **CASA**, or a **child advocate**, or a **guardian ad litem**."

Gilbert's eyes grew wide. "Is that like a guardian angel?"

Mrs. Hart laughed. "Close enough. I'm going to look after you just like a guardian angel. I'll be there whenever you need me . . . and that's a promise."

COURT APPOINTED SPECIAL ADVOCATE (CASA)
GUARDIAN AD LITEM (GAL)
CHILD ADVOCATE

All these terms mean the very same thing—a special friend who has been chosen by a judge to look out for you and who always has your best interests at heart.

20

Mrs. Hart took them outside to the playground so they could talk privately.

"I still don't understand how you're different from Ms. Casey," Rachel said.

"Ms. Casey is a caseworker for Child Protective Services. That's her job. She has lots of kids to protect and always has to hurry. That's where **volunteers** like me come in. I'm a Court Appointed Special Advocate and I have only two children to protect. Their names are Rachel and Gilbert."

VOLUNTEERS are people who do a job because they care. They don't get paid. They do it for free because they want to help.

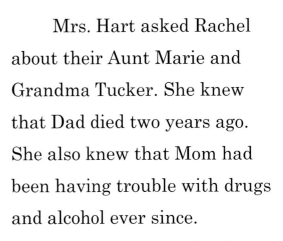

Mrs. Hart asked Rachel about their Aunt Marie and Grandma Tucker. She knew that Dad died two years ago. She also knew that Mom had been having trouble with drugs and alcohol ever since.

Rachel was surprised. "How do you know so much about us?"

Mrs. Hart explained. "Court Appointed Special Advocates learn how to find out important information about the kids they protect. I talked to your old teachers and neighbors. I talked to your attorney ad litem. I talked to your mom and I talked to your mom's attorney. I talked to your new principal. I *will* talk to the judge. And I talked to your soccer coach."

Rachel frowned. "I don't have a soccer coach."

Mrs. Hart tossed her a jersey. "You do now."

A **SUPERVISED VISIT** means another grownup will be there to make sure that you are safe.

Mrs. Hart kept all of her promises. She talked to Gilbert's and Rachel's teachers. Pretty soon they were both in classes they liked better.

Then she set up a **supervised visit** with Mom. They met at the park. Rachel thought it would be wonderful. It wasn't, though. It was sad. Mom tried to act happy. But Rachel could tell she was just pretending. Mom wasn't happy at all. She was still sick.

Two weeks later, they went to the park for another visit. They waited an hour, but Mom never came.

Gilbert spotted a bus and ran to catch it. "I'm going home," he shouted. "I'll bet Mom is there. I'm going to find her."

When Rachel and Mrs. Hart caught up with him, Mrs. Hart said, "If Mom is not here, it means she's still sick. And if she's still sick, you can't go home."

Gilbert cried and cried. Mrs. Hart gave him a hug and reminded him that today was Rachel's first soccer game. When she promised to sit next to him, he finally smiled.

"GO, RACHEL. GO!"

"YEA, NUMBER TEN!"

Rachel heard the cheers and poured on the speed. She made more goals than anybody, and her coach said she was going to be a star.

Gilbert was proud as could be. Still, he knew that Rachel was wishing the same thing he was—*that Mom was here and cheering, too.*

One day Mrs. Hart invited the Lins to bring everybody downtown for a tour of the courtroom. She wanted them to see where the attorneys, the caseworkers, and the Court Appointed Special Advocates gathered to talk to the judge.

The kids took turns sitting on the judge's bench—which was really a chair. Gilbert looked out over the courtroom. "I guess the judge sits up this high because, of all the people in the room, the judge is the most important."

A voice in the back of the room spoke. "Nope. Sometimes the most important people in the courtroom aren't even *in* the courtroom. The most important people in the courtroom are *you*, the children we protect."

Mrs. Hart introduced everyone to Judge Wise. Judge Wise was nice and showed them where all the people of the court sat. He even posed for a picture so they would all remember their field trip.

A few days later Mr. and Mrs. Lin invited Mrs. Hart to join the foster family for a day in the park and miniature golf.

Later that afternoon, Mrs. Lin looked at her watch and said, "We'd better start home. Ms. Casey is coming by for her monthly visit. Mrs. Hart, why don't you come for coffee and say hello?"

As soon as they got home, Rachel and Gilbert sneaked off to the shed to check on Spud. *But Spud was gone*! He had pushed away the board that covered the hole.

Gilbert pointed to Spud's empty food and water bowls. "Oh, no! It was my turn to feed him this morning and take him out. But we left so early, and we were having such a good time . . . I forgot."

Rachel bit her lip. "Poor Spud. I forgot, too."

"What are we going to do?" Gilbert wailed.

Spud was alone and hungry somewhere. Rachel knew they needed help. Grownup help. But if the Lins found out how sneaky she and Gilbert had been, they might make them leave.

Mrs. Hart said she would be there when Rachel and Gilbert needed her. Did she really mean it? Would she keep her promise?

Rachel sure hoped so. Mrs. Hart was their only chance.

Rachel told Mrs. Hart all about Spud. "What should we do?" she asked in a small voice.

"You should tell the Lins right away," said Mrs. Hart.

"What if they make us leave?" A lump rose in Rachel's throat. She didn't want to leave now. She felt safe here. Gilbert was happier. It was fun having so many brothers and sisters.

Mrs. Hart took Rachel's hand. "Whatever happens, I'll be by your side and on your side. I promise."

Rachel told the Lins the whole truth and then watched nervously while they whispered with Mrs. Hart. When Mr. Lin turned to the children, he frowned and his voice was stern. "I have something important to say, and I don't want any tears."

"Oh, no!" Rachel thought. "He's going to kick us out."

Mr. Lin smiled. "We don't have time for crying because we all need to get to work and find Gilbert's dog!"

Rachel couldn't believe it. The Lins weren't going to make them leave. They were even going to help find Spud!

Mrs. Lin barked out orders like a general. "Gilbert, make some posters. Vernon, find the flashlights. Rosa! Maria! Stop pinching each other, and Saraaaa...aaaahhhhhHHHHHH CHOOOOO! Will you please find me a tissue?" She laughed. "I guess just talking about dogs makes me sneeze."

Rachel smiled up at Mrs. Hart. "Did you ask the Lins not to kick us out?"

Mrs. Hart winked. "Let's just say I put in a good word for you. After all, that's what guardian angels are for."

They divided into search parties to look for Spud.

Gilbert felt miserable. "Spud was my dog. I didn't take good care of him. No wonder he ran away. He probably hates me now."

Rachel chewed her lip. Locking Spud inside a shed by himself wasn't the right way to take care of him or keep him safe. That was sort of what Mom did to her and Gilbert. She locked them in the house and left them alone. Even so, they still loved her. They still wanted to be with her. That made Rachel think . . . .

"Gilbert," she said. "Remember the day you tried to get on the bus? You wanted to go find Mom even though Mom wasn't taking real good care of us. I'll bet you anything Spud wasn't running *away* from you. I'll bet he was trying to get *back* to you. If Spud wanted to get into the house and find you, he would have to go through all those bushes. Come on. Let's look!"

Sure enough, there was Spud hiding in the bushes. The minute Spud saw Gilbert, he came running out and jumped into his arms.

Rachel shouted loud enough for the whole neighborhood to hear.

"WE FOUND HIM!

WE FOUND HIM!"

Ms. Casey arrived just as they brought Spud into the house. Mrs. Lin greeted her with a big, "AHHHHHH CHOOOOOO!"

Spud let out a series of happy barks. "ARF! ARF! ARF!"

Ms. Casey's glasses slipped down her nose. "My goodness! Where did this cute dog come from?" She scratched Spud under the chin.

Mrs. Hart explained everything to her. When she got to the end, Gilbert asked, "What's going to happen now? I love Spud, and he loves me."

When Rachel's mom left her and Gilbert alone and didn't make sure they were safe, that was **NEGLECT**.

REUNIFICATION is when kids go back to where they lived before CPS moved them.

Ms. Casey took Spud and held him in her lap. "I'm afraid what we have here is a case of **neglect**. If Spud were a child, I would take him to a temporary foster home. Then, if Gilbert showed me that he could take care of him properly, we would arrange for **reunification**."

Mrs. Hart smiled. "Do you think it might be possible to find Spud his very own foster home . . . just for now?"

"As usual," said Ms. Casey as Spud licked her face, "I have an idea . . . ."

Summer arrived and was full of exciting events.

Ms. Casey became Spud's temporary foster mother. She took him to work with her. He helped by making the kids who came to the CPS office laugh.

Gilbert started **therapy**. He talked to a therapist about all the things that were happening. He drew pictures for the therapist and smiled more and more every day.

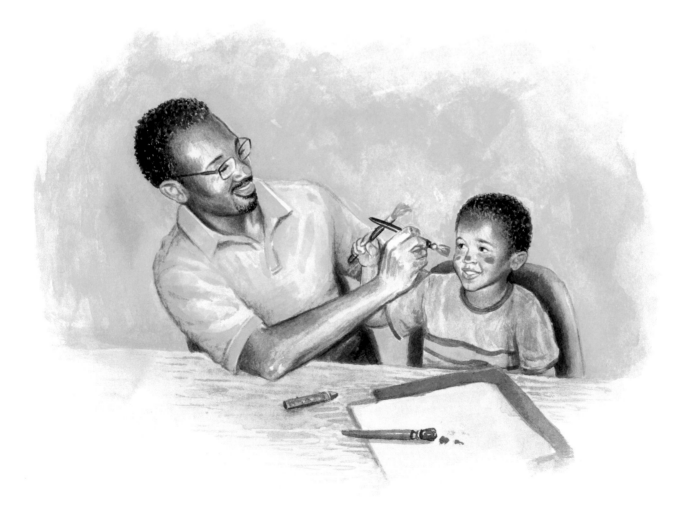

Vernon's parents got out of jail and took him home for good. They sent the Lins a note that said, *"Dear Mr. and Mrs. Lin, thank you for taking good care of Vernon. We are going to be a Super Family from now on."*

Maria and Rosa went to live with their aunt on a ranch in Montana.

And Sarah got some new parents. *Really* nice ones. Mr. and Mrs. Lin! They legally adopted her, and her placement became permanent.

But the *most* exciting event of the summer was Rachel's birthday. Mrs. Hart arranged a party for Rachel before Vernon and the twins left. Rachel made a wish and blew out the candles on her cake. This year her birthday wish came true *right away*. The door opened and in walked . . .

"MOM!"

Mom's eyes sparkled and her face shone. She really was happy. She wasn't pretending.

Mom said Mrs. Hart had helped her get into a hospital so she could get well. Now she was taking classes to learn how to be a better mom. "I'm going to work hard to make our home safe and happy. I'm going to prove to the judge that I can take care of you."

"When can we come home?" Gilbert asked.

Mom put her arms around them. "I don't know that yet. But I do know this—you and your sister are safe. You're healthy. And you have a Court Appointed Special Advocate with a big heart. That's enough to make me happy . . .

at least . . . *just for now.*"

The ~~End~~

the beginning

Glossary

Abuse–Some kids are removed from their homes because they are being *abused* (harmed or injured). There are different kinds of abuse, but the most common kinds of abuse are *emotional abuse, physical abuse,* and *sexual abuse.*

Ad litem–Your attorney *ad litem* or guardian *ad litem* is an attorney or guardian who has been appointed (chosen) by a judge to help you with your case.

Adoption–This is when you get new parents and you become a permanent member of their family. In the story, Sarah was *adopted* by the Lins.

Advocacy Coordinator–The person who makes sure your Court Appointed Special Advocate has the information he or she needs to help you.

Advocate–Someone who speaks up for you and protects you.

Attorney–Same thing as a lawyer. The job of your attorney is to be your advocate and speak for you in court. Your attorney will speak to the judge as if he or she were standing in your shoes. Everyone involved in the court system has an *attorney*—you, your parents, your guardians and even offices like Child Protective Services (CPS).

Attorney ad litem–A special attorney who has been appointed (chosen) by a judge to speak for you about your case. In the story, Rachel and Gilbert did not have an attorney, so a judge appointed Mr. Zapato to be their *attorney ad litem* and stand in their shoes.

Bailiff–A police officer who makes sure that the people in the courtroom behave.

Best interest–The judge will decide what is *in your best interest* (what is best for you). Your advocates and guardians help the judge to know what that is.

Bench–The judge's seat in the courtroom is called *the bench* even though it is really a chair.

CASA–See *Court Appointed Special Advocate* and *National Court Appointed Special Advocate Association.*

Case–Your *case* means your situation.

Caseworker–The person who knows all about your case (your situation), and works to make it better. In the story, Ms. Casey is a *caseworker* for Child Protective Services (CPS).

Child Advocates, Inc.–An office in Houston, Texas, where volunteers learn how to be Court Appointed Special Advocates (CASAs) for kids.

Child Protective Services (CPS)–Every city has a Child Protective Services office. In some cities it might be called something else, but the job of the people who work there is always the same—to help kids and keep them safe.

Compliance–When you do the things you are supposed to do.

County Attorney–The attorney who speaks to the judge for the people who work in county offices like Child Protective Services (CPS).

Court–The official meeting place where people gather to talk to the judge. The court*room* is the big room where everyone meets. The court*house* is the building. The word *court* can be confusing for kids because sometimes when people say *the court,* they really mean *the judge.*

Court Appointed Special Advocate (CASA)–A special friend and volunteer who has learned how to look out for you while you are in CPS custody. This person is appointed (chosen) by the court (a judge). A *Court Appointed Special Advocate* might also be called a CASA, a guardian ad litem (GAL), or a child advocate. In the story, Mrs. Hart was Rachel and Gilbert's *Court Appointed Special Advocate.*

Court reporter–A person who sits in the courtroom and writes what everyone says in case someone forgets later.

Crime–When a law is broken in a serious way.

Criminal–A person who breaks the law in a serious way is *a criminal.*

Criminal Court–A person goes to *criminal court* because he or she may have broken the law in a serious way. The judge, sometimes with the help of a jury, will decide if that person did or did not commit a crime.

Custody–When someone *has custody of you*, it means a judge said he or she has a legal right to make sure you are safe and well taken care of. In the story, when Ms. Casey removed Rachel and Gilbert from their home, she took them into the *custody* of Child Protective Services (CPS).

Extension–You will be in CPS custody until a judge makes a final decision about where you should live. That should never take more than a year. However, if there is a good reason to wait longer before making a final decision, the judge may grant *an extension.*

Family Court–Families go to court when they disagree and need a judge to help them figure out what to do. *Family court judges* are not there to punish people. They are there to help moms, dads, and kids figure out how to make their families work better.

Family Plan of Service (FPOS)–
A list of things your parents are supposed to do to show the judge they are serious about wanting to take good care of you.

Foster home–If your parents, relatives, or friends cannot take care of you, you might go live in a foster home. A foster home is a temporary home and a safe place. In the story, Rachel and Gilbert went to live in a *foster home.* Mr. and Mrs. Lin were the *foster parents.* Vernon, Sarah, Rosa, and Maria were *foster brothers* and *foster sisters.* During the time they all lived together, they were a *foster family.*

Gallery–The area of the courtroom where people sit and wait for their turn to talk to the judge.

Gavel–A little hammer that belongs to the judge. When the judge makes a final decision, *he bangs his gavel* on the desk.

Guardian–Someone who has the legal right to make sure you are safe and well taken care of. Sometimes a guardian might be the person who takes care of you on a daily basis, like a foster parent.

Guardian ad litem (GAL)–
Sometimes this is the same thing as a Court Appointed Special Advocate. A guardian ad litem is someone who is appointed (chosen) by a judge to look out for you while you are in CPS custody.

Hearings–Every few months many of the grownups involved in your case meet with the judge to talk about how you and your parents are doing. Those meetings are called *hearings.* Even though you may not be there in person, your Court Appointed Special Advocate and attorney ad litem will be there to speak for you and make sure the judge hears what you have to say.

Judge–The person in the courtroom who makes final decisions. Remember, sometimes people say *the court* to mean *the judge.*

Jury–A special group of people who sometimes help the judge make a decision.

Laws–Official rules that everyone has to follow.

Lawyer–The same thing as an attorney—a person who speaks to the judge for you in court.

Legal–When something follows the law, it is *legal.*

National Court Appointed Special Advocate Association (NCASAA)–There are more than 900 Court Appointed Special Advocate (CASA) programs all around the country. These programs teach volunteers how to be Court Appointed Special Advocates (CASAs) for kids.

Neglect–Some kids are removed from their homes because they are *neglected* (not well taken care of). In the story, Rachel and Gilbert's mom *neglected* them when she left them alone for a week. Rachel and Gilbert *neglected* Spud when they left him alone and forgot to feed him or take him outside.

Permanent–The opposite of temporary and just-for-now. *Permanent* means *for always*.

Permanent Managing Conservatorship (PMC)–The permanent legal right to take care of you. In the story, Maria and Rosa's aunt in Montana became their *permanent managing conservator*.

Permanent placement–A place to live that is for always.

Permanency Placement Team (PPT)–The grownups who work together to figure out the best place for you to live. Your team might include your CPS caseworker, your attorney ad litem, and your Court Appointed Special Advocate (CASA).

Reunification–This is when you go back to live with your parents or the people you lived with before CPS moved you. In the story, Vernon's case ended in *reunification* with his parents.

Services–Different kinds of help that you or your parents need in order to be a safe and healthy family: a trip to the doctor, special help with your schoolwork, or therapy.

Shelter–A safe place to go when you don't have another place to stay. Sometimes kids stay in a shelter before they go to a foster home.

Supervised visit–If you have a *supervised visit* with your parents, that means another grownup will be there to make sure you are safe.

Temporary–Just-for-now.

Temporary Managing Conservatorship (TMC)–The just-for-now legal right to take care of you. In the story, Child Protective Services (CPS) had that right when Ms. Casey removed Rachel and Gilbert from their home and took them into CPS custody.

Termination of parental rights–If it looks like your home will never be safe for you, a judge may *terminate your parents' rights*. In the story, Sarah's parents' rights were *terminated* so that she could be adopted by new parents who would take good care of her.

Therapist–Someone who will help you learn about your feelings.

Therapy–A way to understand your feelings. There are different kinds of therapy. Some of the different kinds are *family therapy, group therapy, individual therapy,* and *play therapy* (where you use games, toys, art, music, and dance).

Trial–During a trial, everyone involved gathers in the courtroom to talk to the judge. After everyone has been heard, the judge makes a final decision about where kids will live. A jury may or may not help the judge to make that decision.

Volunteers–People who do a job because they care. They don't get paid. They do it for free because they want to help.

Witness–Someone who goes to court to tell the judge what he or she saw or heard.

Witness box–The place in the courtroom where a witness sits.

The publishers are aware that terms, situations, and procedures may vary from county to county and state to state. Users should feel free to modify the story text and glossary definitions appropriately for their own use. For information on how to do this, please consult our online *Just For Now: Kids and the People of the Court User's Guide* located at www.childadvocates.org. For information about Child Advocates, Inc., please contact them at 2401 Portsmouth Street, Suite 210, Houston, Texas, 77098, 713.529.1396.

Jackie Crowley and Barbara Abell are responsible for *Just for Now: Kids and the People of the Court* book project, a special project of Child Advocates, Inc. Jackie Crowley, a Child Advocate, recognized while working with a family, that Court Appointed Special Advocates needed a communication tool to explain their role to the children they represent. Barbara Abell was honored to partner with Jackie on the book project. Together they worked as volunteer project coordinators for three years to craft a tool that would serve children, advocates, families, and others.

Jackie and Barbara consider it a privilege to have worked with the staff and board of Child Advocates, Inc., the professional team of consultants, writers, artists, editors, the Book Advisory Group, each Court Appointed Special Advocate, and all donors, contributors, and participants in the project. Especially they recognize the contribution of the children and young people who have inspired the book and those who have read and responded to it.

child**advocates**